the element in the room

Acknowledgements

'Less is More first' appeared in Where Earwigs Dare, published by Green Books, 2010.

'It's Not Me It's You' was first commissioned by the Energy Ombudsman, February 2012.

'Copenhagen / Copenhaagen' was broadcast on Radio 4's Saturday Live, December 2009.

This project would not have taken place without the support of The European Development Fund through The Centre for Business and Climate Solutions at The University of Exeter whose aim it is to support small businesses to prepare for the challenges we face from climate change.

First Published by The Quixotic Press for Regen SW 2014.
The Innovation Centre, Rennes Drive, Exeter, Devon, EX4 4RN
– www.regensw.co.uk.

Book design by Momentum Graphics.
Printed and bound in Belgium by Proost on sustainable paper.

Poetry: © Matt Harvey 2014.

Cover illustration: © More than Minutes 2014.

Illustrations: © Tori Dee 2014, © Heidi Ball 2014, © Laura Cochón 2014, © Naomi Ziewe Palmer 2014, © Chloë Uden 2014, © Josie Ashe 2014.

MIX
Paper from responsible sources
FSC
www.fsc.org
FSC® C101807

ISBN 978-0-9927482-1-0

the element in the room

by matt harvey

poems inspired by renewable energy

IN COLLABORATION WITH

regensw
delivering sustainable energy

EUROPEAN UNION
Investing in Your Future
European Regional
Development Fund 2007-13

UNIVERSITY OF
EXETER
Centre for Business
and Climate Solutions

About Matt

Poet, lyricist, enemy of all that's difficult and upsetting, Matt claims that an interest in alternative technology and cutting-edge psychotherapy has led to being involved in a project to develop a car that runs entirely on suppressed rage. They started with a scooter powered by anxiety but it used to speed up when it came to a hazard. He is also a widely published poet who performs all over the country and is often heard on the radio.

www.mattharvey.co.uk

Also by Matt Harvey

- ◆ Here We are Then
- ◆ Songs Sung Sideways
- ◆ Standing Up To Be Counted Out
- ◆ Curtains and Other Material
- ◆ The Hole in the Sum of my Parts
- ◆ Where Earwigs Dare
- ◆ Mindless Body Spineless Mind

For children
- ◆ Shopping With Dad (illustrated by Miriam Latimer)
- ◆ Beastie and the Boys (illustrated by Chloë Uden)

Song Cycles
- ◆ The Songbook of Unsingable Songs (composer Stephen Deazley)
- ◆ A Little Book of Monsters (composer Stephen Deazley)
- ◆ The Same Flame (composer Thomas Hewitt Jones)

Musicals
- ◆ Rumpelstiltskin (composer Thomas Hewitt Jones)

*Dedicated to all those unsung souls
quietly doing what they can to bring
renewable energy to their communities*

Foreword

What can we all do in the face of accelerating climate change? How do we avoid despair, and keep radiating the kind of positive energy the world so desperately needs? How do we harness unlimited human ingenuity and passion in the face of environmental calamity? Well, Regen SW has called in the poets – including the wonderful Matt Harvey, who I've heard on many occasions lifting, entertaining and challenging his audiences.

Through time, poets and artists of all kinds have held a mirror up to society, to help us reflect and engage with some of the fundamental questions we face. Energy cannot be considered from an entirely intellectual perspective; energy generation is the unrecognised beating heart of our culture, the invisible ingredient in our diets, the unseen web that binds us to each other, to our places of work and our places of fun, and to strange people in strange lands. We cannot hope to grasp the magnificent complexity of this without art.

Currently, more than 90 per cent of us purchase our energy from one of the Big 6 energy suppliers, and most of us are not very happy about that. We see their profits rise even as our bills increase, and levels of customer dissatisfaction are at an all-time high.

Community energy takes an entirely different approach, providing communities with an opportunity to take control of their own local energy production, transmission and storage, bringing resilience, wealth and employment, as well as reductions in emissions of greenhouse gases.

Championed by Regen SW, the Community Energy Coalition and a burgeoning army of local practitioners, this sector is growing in the UK, with local energy initiatives springing up across the country. It is the hope of everyone involved, as it is of mine, that this will continue to scale up and play a larger and larger role in moving us towards a more fit-for-purpose energy system.

Matt Harvey's poetry, alongside some wonderful illustrations, will help us to consider some of the questions that this amazing energy revolution presents us with. It makes it all a little more manageable and a little bit more personal. Energy shouldn't be something that is whizzed down the wire or delivered through the gas mains: it's what makes our lives work, and we need to get a whole lot better at co-creating those benefits, for ourselves and our communities. Hopefully, the next time you are faced with a daunting conversation about energy, this little book will provide you with a little pithy material!

Jonathon Porritt

Jonathon Porritt is Founder Director of Forum for the Future www.forumforthefuture.org.

His latest book, 'The World We Made' (£24.95, Phaidon) is available from www.phaidon.com/store

Contents

Introduction by Matt Harvey

As 'Poet in Residence' for RegenSW, I was invited to contemplate energy – in particular renewable energy – and the poems and pictures gathered here are all inspired by energy and our relationship to it. For the record, I wasn't asked to write promotional or propaganda material and, if some of the content suggests otherwise, this simply reflects my own bias and taste. Though having said that, maybe that's why I got the job.

The thing is I do have solar panels on my roof, I've always liked the look of wind turbines, I'd already heard about anaerobic digestion, even if I wasn't sure what it is. So you see I felt well-suited to the role. And was always likely to be enthusiastic.

I attended various events, spoke with many people, and read books and articles. Looking at the work I produced this isn't obvious – but I did! I made a lot of notes. Then I didn't write the poems I thought I'd write. I wrote these ones instead. Well, all but three. Three of these poems are 'crowd-sourced', which is to say I invited individual lines from a crowd of people, taped them together and presto, we'd made a poem. (See pages 24, 44, and 46.) As commissioning editor, I'm entitled to include them!

One of the themes that emerged for me was the possibility of community energy. Communities who co-own their own energy source are significantly more resilient to both economic downturn and climate chaos. Turbines and solar panels are less intrusive when you part-own them and they're keeping your white goods humming.

I feel I've barely scratched the surface of renewable energy, in fact I'd hesitate to go that far: I'd say I've lightly brushed the surface, tickling it a little on the way. None of these words – or pictures – are intended as a 'last word'. They are intended for your pleasure and interest and to provoke discussion. I'm hoping some of them will be set to music. Seriously.

I want to thank the Regen team, who were open and kind, and say a particularly warm thank you to Chloë Uden who engineered the residency with tact and tenacity and supported it with energy, enthusiasm and aplomb. She also had the imagination to bring in brilliant illustrators, Tori Dee, Heidi Ball, Laura Cochón, Josie Ashe, Naomi Ziewe Palmer and More than Minutes.

I'm proud to share these pages with them, their wonderful artwork transforms this from a record of the residency into something more than the sum of its parts, collaborative and alive.

We hope you enjoy it.

The Element in the Room

*This poem is not to scale. It does not adhere to scholarly
standards or scientific exactitude. Its only apology is to Dr Seuss.*

on a blustery day, breezing in from the West
a gust is persuaded to stay as a guest

then a biddable beam, an amenable ray
that was just shining through is invited to stay

Element 1 and Element 2
would like to come in and say How do you do?

tucked in behind sockets they're lurking for certain
they're clustered in pockets behind the neat skirting
so keen to get heating and lighting it's hurting

they've careered along cables at speeds close to thought
now they're ready to caper, to dance and cavort

Element 2 and Element 1
want to get busy, they want to have fun

then the Big Switch is flicked and the Elements flock
zoom in and illumine the digital clock

and hickory dickery, ever so quickerly
emanate oodles of bright electrickery

the charge is at large that was hid in the grid
there's juice on the loose that will do as it's bid

put whizz in our widgets and frost in our fridge
it's a beautiful thing when the elements come
flat screens glimmer, white goods hum

the Elements animate every appliance
channel the sun and the wind like a séance

it's sort of like magic but mostly like science
the pot and the kettle have formed an alliance

the room is alive with the jiving of joules
they gavotte with the gadgets they tango with tools

the toaster is toasting, the shaver is shaving
the rotisserie roasting, the microwave waving

tumble dryer tumble drying
de-humidifier de-humidifying

Henry the Hoover is out on manoeuvres

the radio rolls out a popular song
the waffle iron goes on and on and on

our home is where the megahertz is
the blender blends, the teasmaid curtsies

scampering amps do the waltz of the volts
then the main fuse goes – *fhfzzz* – and everything halts

Element 1 and Element 2
have died!? – what are we going to do????

Element 2 and Element 1
have left the building, upped and gone

nobody pouts and nobody panics
we trust in the *First Law of Thermodynamics*

Energy cannot die – it's just redeployed

it can't be created, it can't be destroyed
it can't be frustrated, it won't get annoyed

it can't be upset, it can't get in a mood
but it can be renewed and renewed and renewed

can be scooped from the sky, can be sieved from the sun
and then ushered inside – though we've hardly begun

to begin, in fairness, to harness the furnace
or funnel the furies in earnest

we will never run out, there is always enough
you can't run out of physics and science and stuff

and the one thing we'll never
run out of is weather

and the weather won't ever – no, not ever, EVER –
the weather won't run out of puff

SAVE ELECTRICKERY

THE
EVOLUTION
OF POWER

YE OLDE
CHARGER

CONTEMPORARY
CHARGER

CHARGE ONLY WHEN REQUIRED

Switch off
when not in
use

SUCCESS!

An Unchanging View

On doorsteps, in driveways, function rooms, civic halls
Comes the sound of the banging of heads against walls
There's nothing to say there's no dance they can do
In the face of 'my Right to an Unchanging View'...

Part I

as a future technology it has potential
but why can't the structures be more ornamental?

I'm as green as the next person, some would say greener
I think fracking's obscene but I'll say what's obscener:

it's not *just* about facts, it's as much about feeling
to change someone's view is the worst sort of stealing

there's so much in life that's outside one's control
but my views are my own – that's how I roll

and whatever you think be assured *you don't know*
the length of the shadow your structure will throw

the ripples go further than you can suppose
there are forces at work... *Taps side of nose*

I'm not saying I know – I'm just saying

and my question is this: What's in it for you
to challenge my right to an unchanging view?

Hmmm?

17

An Unchanging View II

I don't say I agree, but there's plenty of folks
who'll tell you this 'Climate Change' thing is a hoax
not exactly a hoax, but, you know, not proved
has the ice disappeared? Or has it just moved?

I'm not saying I know – I'm just saying

and let's not forget that last Winter it snowed.
it's a myth, do the maths, Mr Smith down the road
– a retired engineer I'm reliably told –
he's been to the Arctic. It's still really cold

no, we don't 'throw out science' – we just pick and choose
when it comes to our right to our unchanging views

An Unchanging View III

it's so inefficient, a terrible waste
most of the power goes back out to space
I read how the energy all leaks away
most of it's lost, at least that's what they say
it's here in the paper – if it isn't true
why don't the solar-tide-wind people sue?

a friend of a man who I actually know
met man on a train who confirmed it, SO

look, I don't reject things just *because* they are new
but I do have a right to an Unchanging View

A Radiant Romance

To fly so far, so fast
And land so gently

Upon a panel on planet Earth

Eight and a third minutes old
And worth its weightlessness in gold

Fallen, faded and cooled

Then to be told,
'Oi photon. Get your coat on.
You've been pulled'

Breaking News

Reports reaching us of a massive sun spill
off the Devon coast... have been confirmed.
And we go now to our reporter on the ground:
Jennifer Willis, what can you tell us?

Well, Hugh, this is quite extraordinary –
visible rays of pure almost liquid sunshine
are quite literally spilling *as I speak* across the coastline
and dancing like ephemeral emeralds
upon the trembling surface of the sea itself.

Did no-one see this coming, Jennifer? The Met Office...?

We can't say we had no forewarning Hugh,
given what has been happening every day, really,
since the dawn of time,
an incident of this magnificence was inevitable.

So this is not the first 'spill' of this scale?

Absolutely not – but that doesn't lessen its impact.
We simply weren't prepared, Hugh,
for the overwhelming sense of, um, of, uh...
I don't know the word...
...Beauty?

That is certainly one word, Hugh. A spokesperson for the
Department of the Environment who didn't want to be
named – or touched – said:

"Whoa. When I see something like this it just...I don't
know... it kind of... makes me question *everything*".

It's thought that the clean up operation will be over by dusk.

It's hard to believe people will simply go back to their normal lives as if nothing has happened.

Meanwhile the awesome beams of dilute gold
continue to wreak their quiet, incandescent havoc.

Traffic is slowed,
jaws are slack,
and literally thousands of sea-birds
dazzled.

This is Jennifer Willis, in the South West,
touched by beauty.

Solar Panel *(Crowd-sourced at Bournemouth Renewable Energy Marketplace – 18th June 2013)*

Shiny summer sponge
Man's clumsy copy of the leaf
Dappled sunlight shining gently for the world
Solar power pays by the kilowatt hour
Have solar not polar
You are smart and shiny and silently elegantly you turn
sunshine into electricity
Solar PV, makes me happee, when the sun shines,
                                    blows my mind
Solar energy is amazing, woooooo!
Sunny side up!
It really enhances 15th century cottage roofs
Sun and air for your home to wear
You can't tax the sun and with solar you can earn a tidy sum
DNO – Friend or foe?
I can't see why there is not PV on every roof
Longing for the black slap of sun on every roof
Hoist the flag of energy freedom: Hail to the solar pv panels
Solar power, a gift from the gods

crowd
sourced
matt & friends

SHINEY SUMMER SPONGE MANS CLUMSY COPY
OF THE LEAF DAPPLED SUNLIGHT SHINING
GENTLY FOR THE WORLD SOLAR POWER PAYS
BY THE KILOWATT HOUR HAVE SOLAR NOT POLAR
YOU ARE SMART & SHINY & SILENTLY, ELEGANTLY YOU
TURN SUNSHINE INTO ELECTRICITY SOLAR PV
MAKES ME HAPPEE, WHEN THE SUN SHINES BLOWS
MY MIND SOLAR ENERGY IS AMAZING WOO
OOOO! SUNNY SIDE UP! IT REALLY ENHANCES
18TH CENTURY COTTAGE ROOFS SUN & AIR FOR
YOUR HOME TO WEAR. YOU CAN'T TAX THE
SUN & WITH SOLAR YOU EARN A TIDY SUM
DNO-FRIEND OR FOE? I CAN'T SEE WHY
THERE IS NOT PVs ON EVERY ROOF
LONGING FOR THE BLACK SLAP OF SUN ON
EVERY ROOF HOIST THE FLAG OF ENERGY
FREEDOM: HAIL TO SOLAR PV PANELS!

SOLAR POWER:
A GIFT FROM THE GODS

WHERE IS THE SMOKE?

COLLABORATIVE THEATRE

Re-tackle projects we dont know much
dont research them & make

WORK LIFE THEATRE

D.N.O
Digital climate Prosator

WHAT DOES RENEWABLE
ENERGY MEAN TO US.....?

Not about what something looks like
but what it means to look at it.

THE MESSAGE NEEDS
TO BE CONSISE

I agree!

No way!

I dont understand

Someones bum?

HOW DO WE GET
THE MESSAGE ACROSS ???

IT'S HARD
TO WADE
THROUGH
LOOKING FOR
WHAT IS FACT
OR FICTION

WHAT'S THIS RENEWABLE
ENERGY THING ANYWAY?
WHY AINT IT ON X-FACTOR?

HOTEL

I assumed
people had
it covered

IT IS FACINATING HOW
SOMETHING SO IMPORTANT
IS CONCERNED
ABOUT BY SO
FEW PEOPLE

it wasn't
forced into
my world
by the media
and powers that be

The Shock of the New

*An exploded moment of the consternation and confusion
turning into recognition and excitement that I experienced on
seeing my first solar farm.*

We turn a corner. Whoa. Slow down. Stop. Jaws drop.
What is this crop?
In ranks across a five acre field –
an immaculately tidy, strangely symmetrical yield

the 1ˢᵗ half-second:
the nimby in me stirs, the nimby brain whirrs
it says: Dark wafers! On guard!
it sees: Darth Vader's business card
the unprepared brain, no clues or hints,
sees an angle-poise posse of glossy super-intelligent plank life
sees alien invasion, the first wave of frighteningly
disciplined after dinner mints

the 2ⁿᵈ half-second:
the nimby brain begins to calm
sees they come in peace & mean no harm
instead sees a huge page of redacted sudoku
sees supplicant place mats, members of the most worshipful
order of coasters
an open air warehouse of flat pack goth garden furniture

the 1ˢᵗ half of the 2ⁿᵈ second:
a light begins to dawn
my skin begins to tingle
as I apprehend their angle
is the optimum to catch the sun

and then I see:
synchronised sunbathers
expectant rectangles
oblongs of elegance
in their very element
siphoning off the sunshine
creaming off the crop of sunbeams

the 2nd half of the 2nd second:
I say Hurray for the array
who with silent simplicity
turn light to electricity
dismay into delight

they're kin to my panels, my own PV
that charge my smartphone, boil my cups of tea

and then I reach epiphany and see:
a choir of angles in a cathedral of stained dark windows,
deep as ink
sacred insatiables whose job it is to drink in radiance

windows to a future not only doable
but so much more renewable
than the *namby pamby Nimby* in me – or anyone –
cares to think

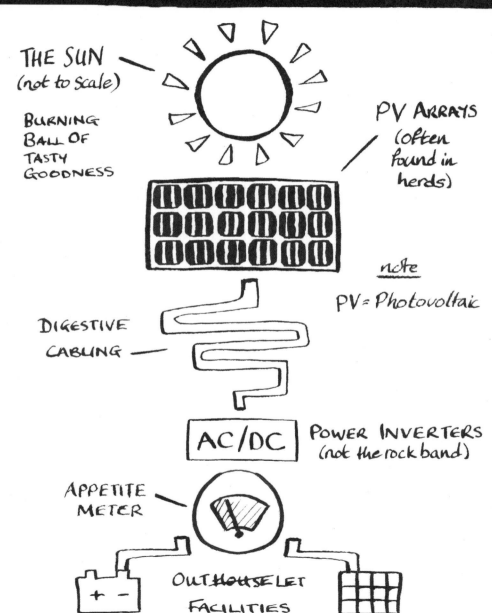

An Unchanging View IV

we have a right to an untroubled bubble
an uncluttered home and an unrattled cage
I know this renewable thing's all the rage

I know clean green energy's come into fashion
I welcome debate and an informed discussion

but what are your sources and where's your compassion?
have you *seen* a kestrel that's suffered concussion?

do you hold nothing dear? Do you really not care?
we can't see them from here.
But *we know that they're there*!

is plotting to blot out the sun not a crime?
and *did* those feet in ancient time?

Pie in the Sky

Put a saddle on a sunbeam
Hang a bridle on a breeze
Ride the tide into the future
Land of Possibilities

They tell me: If you want that kilowatt
You've gotta frack 'n' drill a lot
And then of course you spill a lot
And when I ask them WHY?
They say: Don't let 'em tell you otherwise
Those Greenies tell a pack of lies
When will you people realise
It's all just pie in the sky!
Yee-ha!

Well slap my thigh,
Pie in the sky!
Hi de hi and Ho de ho
It's the high-wide sky-pie rodeo

And I say: If the sky can provide
Gee, that's kinda nice of it
If there's pie in the sky
Then cut me a slice of it

Serve me up a plateful
I'll be glad and I'll be grateful
Earth, water, wind 'n' fire are my dream team
Let's tap the to-ing and the fro-ing
Bag the beaming and the blowing
Milk the movement of the ever-flowing stream
Yee-ha!

So frack me no fracture
And drill me no well
And nuke me no reactor
'Cos I'm goin' for to dwell

In the Land of Possibility
The Land of Ingenuity
Exploiting every property
Of earth, sea, wind and sun
It puts the fill in my philosophy
A sigh in my psychology
Adds meat to meteorology
An' I guess it's kind of fun (Yee-ha!)

In the land where the sky can provide
Yee ha!
In the land where the sky's made of pie
Yee ha!

Because the reckoning is beckoning
The planetary auditors
Are reeling every second in
There's flooding and there's shortages

Put a saddle on a sunbeam
Hang a bridle on a breeze
Ride the tide into the future
Land of Possibilities

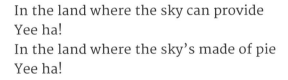

Invocation

By the briskness of the breezes, by the freshness of the days
By the churning of the seasons and the parting of the ways

By the fleeting feral forces we can tap but cannot tame
By the scraping of the barrel, by the fanning of the flame

By the milking of the movement of the waters and the wind
By the deep recurring rhythms regulation can't rescind

By the rhythms of refusal, by the beating of the drums
The complexity of physics, the simplicity of sums

By the ordinary miracle, every minute every hour
By the muscle in the molecule, the pervasiveness power

By the measure of the treasure that will always pass us by
By the awesome orphaned portion of the wide, wide sky

By the planning applications by the placard in the hand
By the opposition's passion, by the curving of the land

Let the blessing of the heavens and the good from underground
Meet completely in the middle in the country and the town

May the blessing be accepted, may we know it isn't wrong
To welcome in the guest who's waited patiently so long

By everything that flickers or flies into a rage
By the twist in all our knickers, by the rattle in our cage

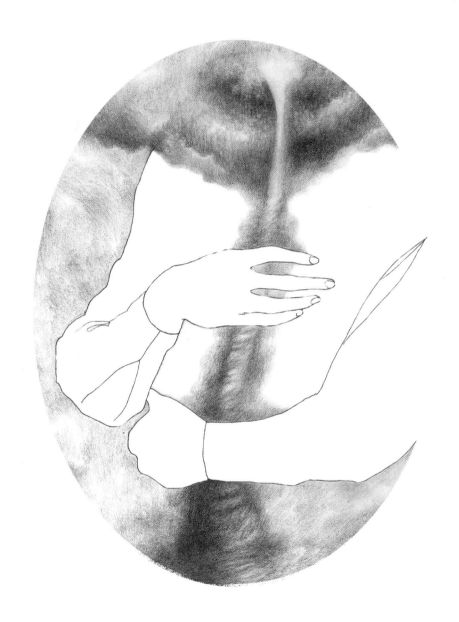

By the facts we're forced to muster in defence and in attack
By our belief in all our bluster, by the monkey on our back

By the throbbing in the temple, by the fury and the fuss
By the bridge across the chasm all the way from Them to Us

By the health and by the safety, by the calculated risk
By the energy encased in our sun's ever-slipping disc

By the gifts we take for granted that may one day be withheld
By the many trees we planted and the many more we felled

By the curbing of the carbon, by the scarring and the stains
By the carbon in the garden, by the flooding of the plains

By the leaking of the data by the sneaking of the peek
By the future we're afraid of and the future that we seek

May we mine the seams of sunshine, trap tornadoes in our nets
May our account come into credit as we pay off our regrets

Let the energy be harvested and gathered safely in
Let the argument be ended, let the reckoning begin

Civil Dispute, Uncivil Tongue

there's an energy inside us, buried deep
which, once awake, is hard to quell or curb
it isn't minded to go back to sleep
a nerve's been touched that lay long undisturbed

though neutral, with no ideology
it grows between what's said and what is heard
triggered by immigrant technology
a yawning gap, abysmal and absurd

like all raw energy it can transmute:
enthuse, freeze, argue, burn with fierce intensity
turn smiles to growls, debate into dispute
in defence of hearth, home and identity

it's power is visceral, it's fight or flight
and always generates more heat than light

Less is More

Can less be more, can more be less?
Well, yes and no, and no and yes – Well, more or less...

More bikes, fewer cars
Less haze, more stars

Less haste, more time
Less reason, more rhyme

More time, less stress
Fewer miles, more fresh (vegetables)

Fewer car parks, more acres of available urban soil
More farmers' markets, less produce effectively marinated in
crude oil

Less colouring, more taste
More mashing, less waste

Fewer couch potatoes, more spring greens
Fewer tired tomatoes, more runner beans

More community, less isolation
Less just sitting there, *more participation!*

More stillness, less inertia
Less illness, more Echinacea

More wells (not oil ones, obviously), fewer ills
Fewer clean fingernails, more skills

More co-operation, less compliancy
Less complacency, more self-reliancy

Less competition, more collaboration
Less passive listening, *more participation!*

Less attention defic..., more concentration
Less passive listening, *more participation!*

(Less repetition)

Less of a warm globe, more a chilly one
More of a wise world, fewer parts of CO_2 per million

Less stress-related cardio-vascular and pulmonary failure
More nurturing quality time in the company of a favourite
clematis or dahlia

More craftsmanship, less built-in obsolescence
More political maturity, less apparently-consequence-free
extended adolescence

More believed-to-be-beautiful, known-to-be-useful *things*
Less cheap, pointless, petroleum-steeped *stuff*

So Yes, less is more – and enough's enough

The Ballad of Further Down the Line – Part I

We left behind the them and us –
divisions in the villages,
uncivil tongues and civic fuss,
the laws of privilege –

to tax the molecules that rush
and pay their dues without a fuss
that rush for no good reason, but
the laws of physics say they must.

The energy that's everywhere –
we took its measure, learned its worth.
We pluck it from the vivid air,
we suck it from the living earth.

Now panels tilt and turbines stand
– familiar reassuring sight –
around the town, across the land
there will be heat and light tonight

And laid in fields or stood in rows
slim sentinels stand surety –
exposed as they themselves expose
the myth of landscape's purity.

On country acre, city roof
alert, unblinking compound eye –
and standing tall without excuse
regret–me–nots against the sky.

An Unchanging View V

what's 'true' is what's carved in the bones and the heart
so, what do I know? Where do I start?

widely known side effects don't get a mention:
they cause social division and family tension
birds get confused, sheep get depressed
and no-one in twenty miles gets any rest

in spite of all this do you still think it's best?
really?

soufflés won't rise, there are more traffic jams
there's a drop in the pass rate of piano exams

I'm simply expressing legitimate doubt
no, it's your turn to listen, it's my turn to shout
your reasoned rebuttals can melt in your mouth
anyway – none of the land around here faces south

correct me if I'm wrong – I can take correction
not one of these turbines has stood for election
it's undemocratic, they're not very nice
they lower house prices, they throw lumps of ice

when the wind's quicker you get shadow flicker
fit people get fits and sick people get sicker
you don't seem concerned, don't you share my revulsion?
do you *like* seeing pensioners having convulsions?

An Unchanging View VI

if you're going to quote figures and point to a graph
I think you'd better speak to my Other Half

his conclusion's conclusive, you can depend on it.
that's why it's a 'conclusion' – there's an end of it

you've picked the wrong fight and you haven't a clue
and we have a right to an unchanging view

these plans were not passed by a panel of peers
and our rights are enshrined in the depth of our fears

in the lines on our foreheads, the crease in our trousers
the deeds of our forebears, and the deeds of our houses

I know what I know in my bones & my bowels
anyway, what have you got against owls?

43

Turbines are Beautiful

(Crowd-sourced at Exeter Renewable Energy Marketplace – 19 March 2013)

Turbine trees, tall and sleek
White cranes talking with the wind
Light majestic mills
You turn my head, and turn my head

Friendly sentry standing on a hillside giving us power
Bladed beauties, air cleavers
Daddy! Look, a windy bine!
What, no cooling towers?

Walkers in white, string strong, day and night
When the wind blows the energy flows
Are these steel totems the future... who knows?
Quixote's foe in minimilist guise

Slowly turning electric stars
Leading the magi who knows where
Turbine: "Why do you stare at me and not my pylon cousin?"

A giant metal whomping willow – magician or dark lord?
Harnessing nature or annoying the hell out of people?
Rich people don't like wind turbines, they spoil THEIR views
It would be great if the turbines were made in the UK
and in colours other than grey

Three blade knife
Elegant Catherine wheel of delight
Dynamic majestic electric
enchanting and peaceful and hypnotising
Catch the breeze to make a spark flow

Wind is the only weather that can cause insanity

White sculpture, whirling power on a pole
The spin doctor's healthy option creating rotation for the nation

No matter how much energy you take from the wind today,
there is still exactly the same amount left for tomorrow
A win win, wind wind situation

Elegant, slender, wind harvesters
Sculpted seductive emotive endless beautiful

I'm a big fan :-)

crowd
sourced
matt & friends

The Effluent in the Room (Crowd-sourced at launch of

Communities Living Sustainably in Dorset Climate Week 2013)

Ribbons of gushing, rushing flows
Gurgling and sluicing, diverting and engaging
Foaming and spuming, splashing and dribbling
Drains, network of pipes which flow to who knows where –
But do we care? We should!
Underground, unseen, essential, unnoticed unless blocked.
As a drain, not for the first time, I can no longer cope
I drink rain but do not allow it to be taken away.
Instead I hold it and it overflows.
Glittering gurgling vortex, beaching detritus as the whorls ebb
Open mouths, sated by the heavens, our salvation?
Busy, hungry, tired drains
The drains gurgle like a baby after it's had its milk.
Glug, glug, glug and now its beginning to stink
Drains do not discriminate. From muddy run off to chip fat.
Greed's emetic tunnels.
Blocked drains cause floods, which bind communities together
Gurgling, bubbling, too much water, overflowing, spilling over
Swallowing sewage and spewing it out again
Mysterious brown objects floating around
Keep it clean – Spare the rod and spoil the drain
Never-mind the rain in Spain landing on the plain, let's talk
Somerset, plain, insane no room down the drain
There are no drains in the drive that's washed
away by the flood to 3 feet deep mud
The drains in rain will flood again
Drains are necessary.
Drains sustain the balance of life
Drains: Water way to go!

crowd
sourced
matt & friends

WIND TURBINE COMPONENTS

TREMENDOUS TOWER OF SUSTAINABILITY

NOSE

TURBINE TIGER
(COMPLEX & MAGICAL)

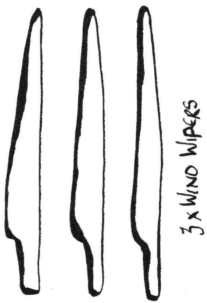

3 x WIND WIPERS

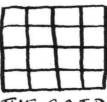

THE GRID

-NOTE
THIS IS A
PICTURE
OF A GRID,
NOT 'THE
GRID!'

The Skywayman

Dick Turbine
Stand and deliver

To Whom Does Energy Belong?

Totnes Renewable Energy Society (TRESOC) issued a share offer in spring 2014 with the opportunity to invest up to £1.5 million into six hydro and roof mounted solar PV projects, offering a collective return of £136,000 per year over 20-30 years.

To whom does energy belong
The energy that's everywhere?
To you, to me, to anyone
Who'll back TRESOC and buy a share

It flows from those who engineer
The means, put physics to the test
Tap elements from far and near,
To all those willing to invest –

Invest in schemes and sweet techniques
Both cutting edge and nothing new
For modern geeks *and* Ancient Greeks
Admire an Archimedes Screw

The spin-off of the river's flow
A silver lining of the cloud
Discreet skim from the sun's warm glow
Embezzlement that is allowed

Afraid don't be to use the Force
It's ethical as you could wish
And close at hand and free at source
It's clean, it's green, it's kind to fish

Affords the fuel-poor, cash-strapped
(Whose rooftops catch the solar rays)
A benefit that can't be capped
Except by clouds and shorter days

For when it shines and when it pours
– On one or both we can depend –
The good accrues to you and yours
When you're TRESOC's all-weather friend

So join the push to prime the pump
Put pounds and pennies in the pot
Prepare to take the plunge and jump
And generate the Megawatt!

Ensure this share floatation floats
– A buoyancy aid for everyone –
Unfurl your twenty-one pound notes
Step up, plunge in, splash out, shine on

HYDROELECTRICITY

RECIPE RECIPE RECIPE

STEP 1. TAKE ONE RESERVOIR FULL OF WATER

STEP 2. PRE-HEAT THE TURBINE-ASSISTED GENERATOR

STEP 3. RELEASE THE WATER INTAKE

STEP 4. TURN UP THE TURBINE TO FULL FLOW

STEP 5. POWERHOUSE UNTIL GOLDEN BLUE

STEP 6. DRAIN EXCESS WATER INTO THE RIVER

STEP 7. SERVE ON A BED OF POWER LINES

DAM

RECIPE RECIPE RECIPE

HYDROELECTRICITY

A Partially Submerged Person in Somerset Makes an Implicit Link Between Extreme Weather Conditions and Climate Change Whilst Hoping the Latter may be Mitigated by Investment in Renewable Technologies

I want to go renewable
So my streets are less canoeable

The Ballad of Further Down the Line – Part II

We'd said that we would mend our ways
– a promise made, a promise kept –
and squeeze the juice from all the days.
Adjust, adapt, accept.

We learned in time to simmer down,
to slow the mad, relentless burn.
Now on the edge of every town
the turbines turn.

The patch-up process has begun,
we came to tolerate and trust
their quiet cartwheels' steady hum.
Adapt, accept, adjust.

We felt the heat, we felt the pinch
and seized the opportunity –
we shuffled inch by grudging inch
toward community.

We shuffled till we overcame
innate inertia that had grown
within our ranks and gained a strange
momentum of its own.

We turned to face the damage done,
address the mess and seal the cracks,
returned to earth and wind and sun.
Accept, adjust, adapt

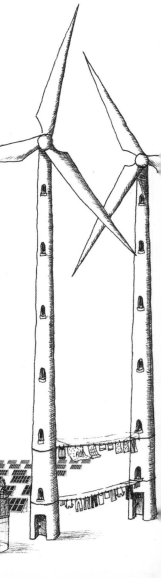

Wind Turbines *(priming the pump for the crowd-sourced poem)*

gale gatherer, gust herder, breeze whisperer
high riser, heaven tickler, bird brainer
onshore – unsure off shore – of course

thrillerblots on the landscape
unflappable flag-poles, looming lollipop sticks
unscaleable energy blossoms, hardy perennial

blooming metal-petalled interlopers
high whirrers, controversy stirrers
stilted spin doctor, blade hummer
standing guard over My Back Yard

Don Quixote monsters, fit to be tilted at
scythe, cutting dine hice prices,

finesser of the wind's fury:
converting crude gusts to cordial kilowatts
energy undrilled for,
that no blood need be spilled for

breath catcher, speed snatcher,
stationary spitfires whose propellers
put the killer into kilowatts
Revolving door into the future
UKIP botherers, swirligigs

Fi, fie, foe fum, here they come with a whirr and a hum,
loved by many and loathed by some, fi, fie, foe, fum

The Not-for-Prophit

The Not-for-Prophit has neither the depth of wisdom nor the elegance of expression of his near-namesake, because unlike The Prophet he was not written by the great Lebanese poet Kahlil Gibran.

And the people gathered to hear the Not-for Prophit, they clustered on the steps of the eco-building where he worked, in Exeter, and said to him, "Speak to us of the Sun."
And he said to them, "Right, so this is a sort of Q & A is it?"
And they said: "It is, yes. So... the Sun?"
And he bellowed: "Ra! Helios! Shamash! Horus! Hunahpu! Lakota!" And they shrank from him, so he said more quietly, "Generations past worshipped the Sun as a deity, as future generations will again. In your own time are those who await a benign extra-terrestrial to come and solve Earth's problems, few yet realize this being is here, has been here all along, ready to help. The time will come when..."
And they interrupted, saying, "Okay, we think we see where you're going with this... Could you speak to us of Wind? In a slightly more downbeat way?"
And he said, "Right, yes, wind. It's very reliable. There will always be wind. And," he added, "it's good to know which way the wind is blowing." He tapped his nose.
And they went, "Ah, you don't just mean the turbines have to face the right way for maximum wind power, do you?"
And the Not-for-Prophit said. "That's right. I mean the winds of change are blowing wind turbines (and other technologies) your way. It's not a question of whether they are coming or at what speed, but where they sit and who owns them."
And they looked at him suspiciously and said, "Hmmm," and

he said, "Perhaps I should say something about community?"
And they said, "Go on then. Speak to us of Community."
And one of them said, "I really don't like the look of turbines."
And the Not-for-Prophit said. "Would it help if they were
your turbines?" And they shook their head, "Nope."
The Not-for-Prophit ignored them and ploughed on, "if you
collectively own them, rather than a company in Belgium,
they become more attractive and you become more part
of a community. Sometimes you don't recognise you're a
community until you act as one."
"Yeah. Right." said the people as one, looking and sounding
pleased with themselves.
"Yeah," said the Not-for-Prophit, "right."
"You sound like some sort of communist," one said.
"But I'm talking about shareholding."
"Well, a capitalist-communist then," said another person.
"We're not comfortable."
"I'm sorry to hear that," said the Not-for-Prophit.
And one of them changed the subject, saying, "Speak to us of
Fossil Fuels."
"What are you like?" said the Not-for-Prophit rhetorically.
"You've only just discovered them, really, and they're two-
thirds gone."
"Not two-thirds." said the People.
"Okay, five-eighths," said the Not-for-Prophit. "I'll tell
you what you're like, you're like tenants who discover a wine
cellar under your home. You've had an amazing party,
stayed drunk for months, trashed most of the
house, and it's just beginning to dawn on you
you'll have to sober up, clean the house and
make more wine yourselves."
"It's not five eighths gone." said the People.

"What about fracking?"

"Huh, talk about scraping the barrel," said the Not-for-Prophit

"Speak to us of Frugality," they said next.

And the Not-for-Prophit said, "Are you sure you want me to speak to you of Frugality?"

And they said, "You're right, let's leave it. I know, speak to us of Carbon."

"We're all carbon-based life forms – how do you mean?"

"You know, Carbon Emissions, CO_2 in the atmosphere, Climate Change. That sort of thing."

And the Not-for-Prophit said: "You don't believe in that climate change stuff do you?"

And they said "But, but... we thought... I mean, we assumed...

And the Not-for-Prophit said: "Just kidding. Of course I believe. The sum of money does not exist that could stop me believing in it."

"Eeeeewwww," said the people, "get you!"

"...which economic note", continued the Not-for-Prophit, "brings me to my point: You could start to charge for carbon."

And the people said, "How do you mean, charge for carbon?"

And the Not-for-Prophit said: "A sum of money per tonne of CO_2. You know, just as you'd charge those who pollute, stain, and otherwise despoil the earth. You live in a money-driven world – so put a price on activity that damages it."

"Okay." they said, slowly. "This might be hard to implement"

"I didn't say it would be easy. A set charge per tonne of carbon emissions would do more to save the planet than any amount of recycling and green poetry anthologies."

"Well," said the people, "we didn't expect you to be so opinionated and political."

The Not-for-Prophit shrugged.

"Any last thoughts?" said the People

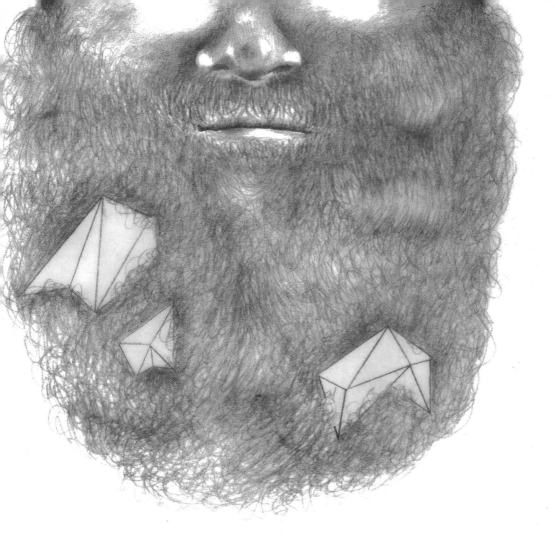

"Don't look a gift-source in the mouth."
And with this the Not-for-Prophit turned and began to climb
the stairs back to his office.
"Are you off then?" asked the People.
"Yes."
And he was.

You Say

You say it's unaesthetic
I say it's kinesthetic

The Art of Finessing a Finer Future by Pruning the Unpromising Petroleum-Based Foliage of the Present

Utopiary

An Unchanging View VII

I've heard all your 'facts', I have gritted my teeth
I've stayed calm and relaxed while I seethed underneath

I've been quite coherent, it's you who's confused
you with so much to gain while I've so much to lose

it's not just my taxes I've paid but my dues
and I am entitled to unchanging views

I'm just sticking up for the natural order
so go back and say to your masters at Mordor

that the jewel in the crown of my message to you
is that I have a right to an unchanging view

yes I do

yes I do

Copenhagen/Copenhaagen

approaching Copenhaagen
we're all hoping that they'll harken
to the Wave and cut the carbon
but will they hide behind their jargon
strike another dodgy bargain
let the seas rise and skies darken
on the road from Copenhaagen

or

when they get to Copenhagen
will they do something surprising
will they be both stirred and shaken
look beyond the near horizon
take a road as yet untaken
while we still can, from Copenhagen

and whether your Copen
is haagen or hagen
here's hoping...

Paris *(Paris hosts the UN Climate Change Conference in 2015)*

so on next year to Paris
will it prove the healing chalice
of the global village parish

will the carbon be discouraged
and the global garden nourished
will we frack or will we flourish

in the shadow of the Eiffel
while the world watches and tenses
will the outcome be so awful
or will we come to our senses
reach agreement and consensus?

will we prosper – will we perish
will the wider world be cherished
après Paris?

briefly:
Paris chalice
nourish parish
perish cherish
frack or flourish?

one worries

It's not Me, it's You

I admit that it appalled me
that day you first cold-called me

but you charmed me, won me over
told me I would be in clover

and I succumbed to your advances
thought: what the heck, I'll take my chances

I told the Doubting Thomases
that you would keep your promises

you'd said that you would care for me
that you'd always be there for me

oh how very wrong of me
I should have thought more carefully

all that warmth and bonhomie
now seems like such hot air to me

for when I called to clarify
the startlingly high tariff I

was on, you proved elusive
and remarkably reclusive
for one so formerly effusive

in breach of all known etiquette
you started playing hard-to-get

left me feeling so much smaller
as if *I'm* the nuisance caller

with designs on *your* affection
which is vexing and perplexing

I don't think it would hurt to see
a bit of old world courtesy

so I'm parting from your company
who's dumping who? You're dumping me

constructively dismissing me
I trust you'll soon be missing me

and then you'll once again change tack
predictably you'll call me back

and find you're waiting in a queue
to hear, when you at last get through

Goodbye.

It isn't me. It's you.

Because the Sun Cannot Unshine

Because the sun cannot unshine
Because the earth's core cannot freeze
The tide is bound to toe the line
Its restless motions never cease

The wind can drop but not unblow
Sun can be blocked but not constrained
Earth can't unspin, nor streams unflow
Because the oceans can't be drained

Because the need is always there
Because the means are all around
Alive within the quickening air
Within the waters, underground

Because a price must yet be paid
For all our craft and artifice
There is a choice that must be made:
The Now price or the After price

Why would we not reap sun, wind, sea
And seek to maximise the crop?
The power is here. Why wouldn't we?
Why on Earth would we stop?

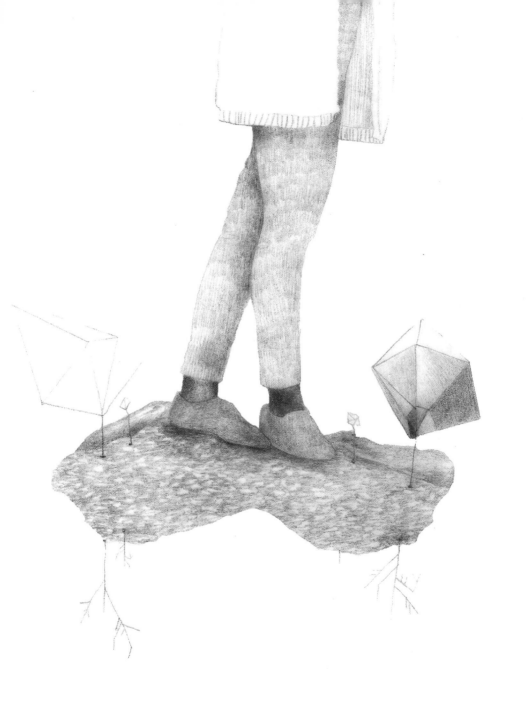

With thanks to our illustrators

Josie Ashe

Josie is an Exeter based artist and designer. She often works with themes related to her background in earth sciences, renewable energy and landscape restoration. Josie's work includes illustrations and bespoke design projects, such as Regen's smart grid pictures. Selected prints of Josie's work are available though her website – www.dododesigns.co.uk

See front and back inside cover.

Heidi Ball

Heidi Ball is from Cornwall, has a BSc (Hons) from Nottingham Trent University and an MA in 'Illustration: Authorial Practice' from Falmouth University. She won the Atlantic Press's Graphic Literature Prize in 2014. Her work draws on a comedic outlook and a love of narrative illustration.

See pages 16, 20, 21, 28, 37, 47, 48, 52.

Laura Cochón

Laura Cochón is a Galician illustrator who specialises in pencil drawings and currently self-publishes and designs illustrated albums and books. She saw the Regen SW project as an opportunity to shed some light through the realm of imagery on a far-reaching issue; the handling of nature's resources.

See pages 33, 34, 57, 59, 69.

Tori Dee

Tori Dee is based in Exeter. She says "This project is not just about the benefits of sustainable energy, it's about challenging our perceptions and the underlying fear of change which lurks in us all. I'm proud to have been a part of it."

See pages 30-31, 40-41, 54.

More than Minutes

A bunch of artists, illustrators and animators who love to make minutes mean more – Regen SW regularly works with this organisation to document events. The front cover for this book was produced during one such event. www.morethanminutes.co.uk

See pages 25, 53 and front cover.

Chloë Uden

Chloë is an illustrator and art producer. She set up The Quixotic Press whilst caught up in the romance of noble deeds and the pursuit of unreachable goals. Chloë also works with Regen SW to generate art and energy projects renewably.

See pages 12, 14-15, 17, 18-19, 29, 43, 63.

Naomi Ziewe Palmer

Energy is important in the lively business of drawing. To Devon-based illustrator (and Creative Writing teacher) Naomi Ziewe Palmer, positive imagery is crucial to communicating the importance of sustainable energy today, because engaging people in green issues is achieved by first capturing the imagination. Naomi makes pictures that are playful, fun and anchored in the magic of childhood.

See pages 23, 49, 60-61, 62.

Old Saying

Keep your friends close
But your energy closer